Douglas Head Ferry
and the Port Soderick Boats

Captain Stephen Carter

Steph C
July 2004

TWELVEHEADS PRESS

TRURO   2003

Contents

Front cover top: KARINA *at Port Soderick in 2002 after modifications to funnel and wheelhouse to return her to more traditional look.*
STEPHEN CARTER
Front cover bottom: SHAMROCK *leaving Battery Pier.*
STEPHEN DEARDEN COLLECTION

TWELVEHEADS PRESS

First published 2003 by Twelveheads Press,

ISBN 0 906294 55 X
British Library Cataloguing-in-Publication Data.
A catalogue record for this book is available from the British Library.

Designed by Alan Kittridge
Printed by
The Amadeus Press, Cleckheaton, West Yorkshire.

Introduction

If you asked a question in a quiz to name an Isle of Man ferry operation which in its heyday carried over half a million passengers every year and operated a fleet of steam and later motor ferries, most would answer 'the Isle of Man Steam Packet Company'. However, it was another locally based concern that once boasted these impressive passenger figures, a ferry service which today is virtually forgotten.

In Victorian and Edwardian times the Isle of Man, and Douglas in particular, was a mecca for holidaymakers from England, Ireland, Scotland and Wales. Apart from the Isle of Man Steam Packet, numerous companies including the Midland Railway and the Liverpool and North Wales Steamship Company ran regular steamer services to Douglas and this town quickly developed into one of the north west's great tourist centres. Much tourist development was centred on Douglas Head, south of the harbour, and in 1896 an electric tramway was opened from there to Port Soderick, a cove three miles south of Douglas that was being developed by the Forrester family and others. On Douglas Head there was an open air theatre with daily black and white minstrel shows, an hotel, various stalls, an open air swimming pool built into a rocky cove at Port Skillion (incidentally the first in Douglas to allow mixed bathing when Douglas Beach was strictly segregated into male and female bathing areas), a camera obscura, a 200 feet high tower with a revolving platform and many other minor attractions. The quickest means of access was by ferry across the harbour and then ascending to the headland on a cable worked incline railway. Visitors to Douglas Head today might find it difficult to visualise just how busy the area was in the days which were the pinnacle of the tourist industry in the island.

Port Skillion. MICHAEL MESSENGER COLLECTION

POINT OF AYRE

RAMSEY BAY

RAMSEY ☐

MAUGHOLD HEAD

ISLE OF MAN

☐PEEL

CONTRARY HEAD

LAXEY ☐

LAXEY HEAD
LAXEY BAY

PORT GROUDLE ☐

DOUGLAS ☐

NIARBYL BAY

DOUGLAS BAY
DOUGLAS HEAD

PORT SODERICK ☐

FLESHWICK BAY

SANTON HEAD

PORT ERIN ☐

CASTLETOWN

☐ ☐DERBYHAVEN

☐
PORT ST MARY

CALF OF MAN

DRESWICK POINT

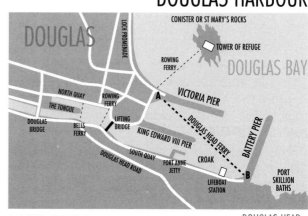

DOUGLAS HARBOUR

A - VICTORIA PIER FERRY STEPS
B - BATTERY PIER FERRY STEPS

4

Chapter One
The early days

The 1860s and 1870s saw a huge increase in the number of visitors to Douglas and much expansion took place with the building of Victoria Pier, Battery Pier, the Isle of Man Railway and a host of other smaller developments and, as described in the introduction, Douglas Head became one of the main entertainment centres of the town. The Isle of Man Government's Harbour Commissioners were by the early 1880s licensing ferryboats to ply on various routes. In Douglas there were ferries across the inner harbour, at the site of the present road bridge. Further up the harbour Bells Ferry ran between North Quay and South Quay. There was also a licensed ferry between Victoria Pier (Peveril Jetty) and the Tower of Refuge in Douglas Bay. But the most important route in terms of passenger numbers was the ferry between Victoria Pier and Battery Pier, which provided access to the attractions of Douglas Head. By 1885 Douglas Harbour Commissioners were offering leases for up to four steam ferries and twelve rowing ferries on this route. Each lessee had to bid for the licence and operate boats that had to be surveyed annually by the Board of Trade or, in the case of rowing or sailing ferries carrying not more than 20 passengers, the local boat inspector (a Harbour Commissioners' officer). In 1885 the Harbour Commissioners issued sixteen licences, steam ferries being operated by four individual owners Burrows, Cowin, Bell and Knox.

In the late 1870s a local man, William Knox, had established an engineering and ship repairing business in Lake Road, at the top of Douglas Harbour, and he must have observed the good business to be had on the Douglas Head Ferry. In December 1883 he applied to the Harbour Commissioners for a licence for a new steam ferry he was building and it was granted on 9 February 1884. In the following year he applied to the Harbour Commissioners for a another licence for a second ferryboat, the *Jumbo*. On 12 August 1884 Knox's appeal for an increase in the number of passengers that the *Jumbo* might carry was rejected the Harbour Commissioners.

By 1888 the Knox family – by this time William seems to have been joined by his sons John and Robert (another son Archibald was a painter and sculptor of some repute) – were involved in another venture, the Douglas and Port Soderick Steam Ship Company which had a fairly large steamer, the *Mermaid*, built at Peel and placed on the Douglas to Port Soderick run. At this time there was no landing stage at Port Soderick and vessels plying to this attractive destination had to land passengers onto the beach by small boat. In May 1888 Knox applied to the Harbour Commissioners to build a pier at Port Soderick but permission was refused, as the they felt it would interfere with the navigation of sailing boats using the bay. However, in February 1889 the Commissioners relented and agreed to a modified plan. Knox was granted permission to build a pier on the north side of Port Soderick beach. But Knox never took advantage of this permission and his vessel continued to land passengers on the beach by small boat. Some years later a landing jetty was built at Port Soderick – and is still in use today. As an aside, at the same Harbour Commissioners meeting in February 1889, Richard Maltby Broadbent applied and was granted permission to build a pier at Groudle Bay, just over a mile north of Douglas. At this time the development of Groudle had not commenced. Broadbent subsequently developed this glen into another major attraction but the pier at Groudle was never built.

In June 1889 the Harbour Commissioners took action against the owner of a small steamer, the *Island Light,* which, it was reported, was carrying passengers between Douglas and Port Soderick but which was unsurveyed and unlicensed.

By February 1890 Knox seemingly monopolised the Douglas Head trade, as the Harbour Commissioners granted him a lease for five years on payment of £220 per annum. No other operator is mentioned. At the same meeting Thomas Forrester, whose family will come to prominence later in this narrative, was applying to the Commissioners to build a pier at Port Soderick but he was informed that Knox had been granted permission and that they could not sanction two piers. It was Forrester who eventually built Port Soderick Pier and henceforth dominated the Port Soderick passenger trade from Douglas Harbour. In the Spring of 1890 Knox erected turnstiles on Battery Pier. Business was booming and it would appear that ferry captains were not averse to overloading at busy times. On the 19 August 1890, the Harbour Commissioners wrote to Knox informing that proceedings would be taken against him should overloading be permitted on his steamers. A truculent Knox retaliated, complaining of berthing difficulties caused by other vessels at Battery Pier. On 5 September 1890 the Commissioners replied to a complaint about overloading on the Douglas Head Ferry from no less a person than the island's Lieutenant Governor Spencer Walpole. They assured the Lieutenant Governor that a prosecution against the lessee of the ferry (Knox) had already been instigated and fines inflicted upon him, following the evidence of their boat inspector (the first boat inspector was George Kelly who had a long career with the Harbour Commissioners, eventually retiring as Chief Harbour Master). By this time Knox was operating four steam ferries on the service: the *Manx Lass* was a conventional single screw steam launch; the *Jumbo* and the *Jingo* were, as far as can be ascertained, double ended ferries, purpose built for the job; and the largest, the *Sambo*, built in 1890, set the standard for future Douglas Head Ferry boats, being double ended with twin screws at either end.

William Knox had additional financial interests in trawlers and the steam tug *Lancashire Lass*, which was used as a general workboat and tug, towing sailing vessels in

Battery Pier, Douglas with the original wooden ferry steps just below the steam crane. The tug and sometimes passenger ferry LANCASHIRE LASS is just leaving the steps while the double ended JUMBO approaches. Lying alongside the pier is an Isle of Man Steam Packet Company paddle steamer – either the PRINCE OF WALES or QUEEN VICTORIA, identical sisters of 1568 grt, built in 1887 by Fairfield. Also the Liverpool and North Wales paddle steamer PARIS. BY KIND PERMISSION OF MANX NATIONAL HERITAGE

and out of harbour and also towing the Douglas Town Commissioners' hopper barge (by which means the town's rubbish was disposed of in the Irish Sea).

The *Lancashire Lass* was, reportedly, later converted to motor and operated as a passenger vessel by the Canipa family, but no records or photographs have been found to substantiate this claim. The *Sambo*, *Jingo* and *Jumbo* – names which reflected the popular black and white minstrel shows which were performing on Douglas Head – were technically very interesting. The *Sambo* was fitted with two compound engines each driving a shaft, which went from one end of the vessel to the other, with a propeller at

The MANX LASS heading for the Victoria Pier, passing a small local cutter and sailing trawlers.
BY KIND PERMISSION OF MANX NATIONAL HERITAGE

Laid up for winter in the River Douglas, alongside the Tongue, are Knox's double ended ferries the SAMBO and JINGO. On the other side of the Tongue is the Isle of Man Steam Packet Company's four funnel paddle steamer BEN MY CHREE – built by Barrow Shipbuilding Company in 1875. She was re-boilered 1884 and fitted with four funnels, instead of the original two. BY KIND PERMISSION OF MANX NATIONAL HERITAGE

each end, so that they had four propellers and two rudders. One shaft would have two right handed props whilst the other two left handed, so that when running in one direction the leading prop would be pulling and the after prop pushing. Why they decided on this unusual design is not clear. There were Mersey ferries with a similar propulsion layout, and apparently by splitting the engines, i.e. running one ahead and one astern, it gave them great turning ability for leaving the often constricted berths without the use of spring lines.

Knox's ferry ventures seem to have been very successful and attracted the attention of other entrepreneurs who were at this time expanding their business interests on the island including: the Isle of Man Tramways and Electric Power Company (later to become the Manx Electric Railway); the Douglas horse tramway; and numerous hotels. Their downfall was an ambitious scheme to purchase every pub and brewery on the Island and then sell the lot, at a considerable profit, to one of the large English breweries. These schemes were all financed from loans from a local bank called Dumbells Bank – a number of the entrepreneurs were also directors of the bank. Here the story becomes more hearsay than written fact – a story passed down by members of the Knox family. Apparently the business syndicate cast covetous eyes on the Douglas Head ferry service and made an offer to William Knox to buy him out. Knox however did not wish to sell and rejected their financial advances. The syndicate then implemented another plan. In 1895 the Harbour Commissioners asked Knox for an increase in the rent for the lease of the ferry rights. Knox, with an arrogance borne of his sense of security, refused to pay any more. So the Harbour Commissioners advertised the lease for let at the end of the 1896 season. The Commissioners had requested an increase of £40, to just £260 per annum and in hindsight this did not seem much. In the event the Commissioners received four tenders for the lease: George S. Cain tendered at £450; A. Taylor and T. Mills tendered £400; Robert Knox tendered £340 (obviously belatedly realising the mistake in not accepting the Commissioners earlier offer); and J. A. Girling tendered £300. The Commissioners accepted George S. Cain's tender subject to receiving his financial proposals and guarantees.

The managing director of Dumbells Bank was a Scotsman named Alexander Bruce and he also held the important and very influential position of the Town Treasurer for Douglas. Bruce was the architect of most of the entrepreneurial schemes on the island but his name did not often appear in connection with them – his interests were hidden behind nominees. The chairman of the Board of Directors of Dumbells Bank was the head of a respected Manx family, William Baring Stevenson of Balladoole. His son William Augustus Stevenson was a member of the

The Sambo at the Victoria Pier ferry steps with two Steam Packet paddlers at the Pier, and queues of landaus (some of which were owned by the author's great grandfather) waiting for passengers.
MICHAEL MESSENGER COLLECTION

House of Keys for Rushen and a member of the Harbour Commissioners. George S. Cain was described as an engineer of the Lake Engineering Works (close to where the Knox business was established in Lake Road) and his middle name, which was not mentioned in the ferry lease tenders, was Stevenson!

By the turn of the century financial backing for some failed development schemes had brought Dumbells to its knees and the bank crashed on 3 February 1900. Several of the bank directors and senior managers were indicted for fraud and false accounting and were later goaled. Alexander Bruce died before he could appear before the courts. William Baring Stevenson and many others were financially ruined as a result.

Chapter Two
The start of something big

On the 12 December 1896 the Harbour Commissioners had a meeting with George S. Cain who brought along with him Mr J. A. Brown, Mr C. W. Coole and Mr Louie Cowin. They told the Commissioners that they intended to form a limited liability company to work the ferry and asked for a lease of fourteen years, instead of the six years advertised, for which they would offer an annual rental of £450 with the addition of a 15% royalty on takings for all passenger carried in excess of 500,000. This was the first indication in official records of how many passengers were expected to be carried. The Commissioners agreed to these terms but subsequently were advised that under the Harbour Acts a lease of fourteen years was beyond their power to grant. So a six year lease was granted but at the end of the first year the Commissioners extended the lease for one year and as this was then done on an annual basis – it was effectively a recurring lease.

The *Isle of Man Times,* 20 February 1897, reported:

The persons who have undertaken the working of the Steam Ferries between the Victoria Pier and the Battery Pier are busily engaged in making arrangements for the forthcoming season. In anticipation of a big traffic, they are determined that the service shall be as perfect as possible. For this purpose they have gone for entirely new and greatly improved steamers, which will not only safely and comfortably transport the passengers, but will also present a comely appearance. On Wednesday the ferry lessees entered into a contract with the Dee Shipbuilding and Engineering Company for the construction of three twin screw steamers specially designed for this type of traffic. These boats will be 66ft 6in long, l8ft wide, and 6ft 9in depth. They are so designed as to float in a very shallow depth of water, so as to enable them to go alongside the piers at low water. They will be constructed of steel, be double ended, and will be fitted with reversible engines of the most perfect modem type, so as to go in either direction with equal ease. One man can work both the engines and steer, and only three men will be required altogether to work each steamer. In order to provide against the possibility of accident, each steamer is divided into six watertight compartments. Throughout, in fact, each boat has been designed and will be built to comply in the strictest sense with the Board of Trade requirements, and each will be capable of carrying from 300 to 400 passengers. Two of the steamers are to be delivered about the middle of May, and the third by July 1st; and the builders are bound by heavy penalties to complete the contract in the specified time. These handsome and commodious steamers will no doubt add another attraction to Douglas as a visiting resort. We understand that the lessees of the Ferries will shortly register their undertaking under the Companies Act, with a capital sufficient for the proper development of the service. We are also informed that it is intended to build on the Battery Pier a commodious shelter house for the accommodation of passengers, if arrangements can be made with the Harbour Commissioners.

On 23 March 1897 the Douglas Steam Ferries Ltd was incorporated in the Isle of Man.

On 27 March 1897 a prospectus was published in the same newspaper. The salient paragraph of its extensive memorandum and articles reads as follows:

> To purchase, take on lease, or otherwise acquire the licence, lease, right and privilege of conveying passengers in Douglas Bay and Harbour, and of plying and running ferry and other boats for hire between the piers, breakwater, and other points and places in the said Douglas Bay and harbour.

The initial investors were John Archibald Brown, publisher of the local newspaper, the *Isle of Man Times*; George Stevenson Cain, an engineer; David Clarke, a builder; Henry Arensberg, a gentleman; Richard Cain, a merchant, whose family later owned the Castletown Brewery; Walter James Brown, a journalist; and William Horrocks, an architect. Between them they owned 1,210 £1 shares of the authorised share capital of £6,000, with J. A. Brown being by far the biggest investor with 500 shares. The company was authorised to have up to 100 shareholders and the remaining shares were quickly taken up, so that by the time of the first annual return in November 1897 there was a full complement of 100 shareholders holding all six thousand shares. During this period there were three calls on the shares: the initial call being for ten shillings; followed by a second call of five shillings; and a final call of three shillings; so the authorised share capital of £6,000 was never fully called and the total subscribed was only £5,400. The list of shareholders covered a wide spectrum of the population and ranged from waitresses to lawyers and doctors. Shareholders were not confined to Manx residents, many addresses in northern England and north Wales appear. Notable in the shareholder's lists were: the Forrester brothers – Thomas and Morris – of Port Soderick, who

The ROSE possibly in the first year of operation 1897. The harbour is crowded with fishing vessels and two Isle of Man Steam Packet paddle steamers are moored at the Battery Pier. There appears to be a crowd waiting at the top of the Battery Pier Ferry Steps and another ferry alongside, which would suggest late afternoon when passengers would be returning from Douglas Head. Note the piano on the starboard side. STEPHEN CARTER COLLECTION

had wide ranging interests in the holiday trade; Mrs Rosie Boni, described as a musician whose family were involved in the entertainment business on Douglas Head; and, not surprisingly, one John Shimmon, the manager of Dumbells Bank and Alexander Bruce's nominee in many ventures. The first manager of the ferry company was William Horrocks.

The newly incorporated company took over the earlier order for the three identical steam ferries, which were already being built by the Dee Shipbuilding Company at Queensferry, Flintshire. These were updated versions of the *Sambo*, being double ended with the same unusual machinery layout. They were delivered under their own steam but not in time to meet the delivery dates for the 1897 season – only two were in service that year and

the late delivery caused a dispute between the ferry company and the shipbuilders. The three new ferry boats were named *Rose*, *Shamrock* and *Thistle*.

The first to be delivered was the *Rose*, which arrived in Douglas by the beginning of June and immediately entered service. However, she quickly disgraced herself by damaging one of her propellers at low water, for which the ferry company blamed the Harbour Commissioners for not providing a sufficient depth of water. She was quickly repaired and returned to service.

The second ferry steamer, the *Shamrock*, was launched on 25 June 1897 by Miss Clark, daughter of David Clark one of the Directors – the first two ferry boats were supposed to have been delivered by May, to start the season. The *Shamrock* didn't arrive in Douglas until 9 July 1897 and her delivery voyage caused great anxiety as she was feared lost on delivery. Under the command of Capt Robinson the *Shamrock* sailed from Queensferry at 3 p.m. on 7 July and proceeded down the River Dee as far as Mostyn where a fresh north west breeze caused them to stay in Mostyn for the night. The following morning they sailed at 3.45 a.m. the weather having moderated. Capt Robinson had a crew of four plus a shipyard engineer on board for the voyage. By 1.30 p.m. the same day the wind had freshened and the sea became very rough. The *Shamrock* rolled heavily and shipped a great deal of water and with no shelter the crew were wet to the skin and frequently up to their waists in water. At 3.55 p.m. they sighted the Calf of Man but then the weather became thick and they lost sight of the land. In a newspaper interview Capt Robinson later stated, 'We were in a rather ticklish position', a masterly piece of understatement. To add to

A fully loaded Shamrock leaving Battery Pier landing barge. Stephen Dearden collection

The Ferry to Douglas Head, Isle of Man.

JWS 200

A busy day at the Victoria Pier. One steam ferry has just left and its place being taken immediately by a second. In the foreground are two of the rowing ferries used on the same route. Moored to seaward of the ferry steps is the Liverpool and North Wales paddle steamer SNOWDON, built 1892.
STEPHEN DEARDEN COLLECTION

the misfortunes and misery, at 5.55 p.m. the circulating pump broke down and it was impossible to work the engines – the *Shamrock* was drifting at the mercy of the seas. Two hours later they managed to repair the pump and were able to continue the voyage. After sighting Maughold Head they eventually arrived at Ramsey Harbour at 9.05 p.m. The crew had to borrow some clothes from the Prince of Wales Hotel whilst their own were drying. At 4 p.m. the following day, the ferry steamer set off for Douglas and arrived at her new home port two and a half hours later. With 120lbs of steam pressure the *Shamrock* could travel at 8 knots but poor coal had reduced steam pressure and the vessel had only just been able to make headway.

The third ferry steamer, the *Thistle*, took so long in delivery that it never arrived in time for the 1897 season and the ferry company entered into protracted litigation with the builders in relation to the penalty clauses. However, even with only two ferries operating, at the first Annual General Meeting of Douglas Steam Ferries Ltd, in November 1897, they were able to report a profit had been made and declared a dividend of 6%. The report of the meeting was somewhat typical of Victorian times, with shareholders congratulating the Directors, Directors congratulating the Superintendent, and everyone congratulating each other – what splendid fellows they all were!

The first Thistle leaving the Battery Pier ferry steps. By this time the wooden steps had been replaced by recessed steps cut into the stonework of the pier and a toll booth was erected at the top of the steps. STEPHEN DEARDEN COLLECTION

Chapter Three
Growth and consolidation

The ferry service under the Douglas Steam Ferries Ltd began in 1897, the season was from Easter to the end of September but in the Isle of Man the main season was really from the last week in May to the beginning of September, about fourteen weeks when everybody involved in the holiday industry would be busy making money.

Things did not always go according to plan and, as might be expected, there were hiccups in the early years. In December 1898 a rowing boat proprietor, James Keenan, was suing Douglas Steam Ferries Ltd for the sum of £2. 10s for damage alleged to have been caused by the ferry steamer *Rose* to one of his boats, the *Gem*. The case for Keenan was that the *Rose* was coming up the harbour early in the evening of 18 August 1897, to shelter from

Douglas Harbour and Fort Ann Hotel, I.O.M

The SHAMROCK arriving at Battery Pier with the original entrance to Douglas harbour behind, flanked by Fort Ann Jetty on the left and the Red Pier on the right. The large imposing building on the left of the photograph is the Fort Ann, for a time the home of Sir William Hilary, founder of the Royal National Lifeboat Institution. In the Croak are moored two visiting sailing and one visiting steam yacht.
STEPHEN DEARDEN COLLECTION

The ROSE leaving Victoria Pier, with the THISTLE approaching, In the background, on the left, is Douglas Head Lighthouse. Port Skillion swimming baths are between Battery Pier and Lighthouse. On Douglas Head are the Camera Obscura, Douglas Head Hotel, the open air theatre and the revolving tower.
BY KIND PERMISSION OF MANX NATIONAL HERITAGE

heavy weather. But she came too early on the tide, ran aground after passing underneath the new swing bridge and then slewed round hitting and damaging a number of rowing boats which were moored in the Double Corner (an area of the Harbour just landward of the Swing Bridge on the North Quay). Before the building of the Princess Alexandra Pier – an extension to the original Battery Pier in the early 1980s – Douglas outer harbour was a dangerous place in easterly winds, and all manner of vessels had to seek refuge above the bridge. Steam Packet steamers often had to put to sea from Peel instead. The ferry company countered the allegation by saying that the rowing boats were moored too far out in the fairway. A great number of witnesses were called, as it was stated that this was in the manner of a test case, as other rowing boats had been damaged in the same incident. The Deemster, Sir James Gell, gave judgement in favour of the rowing boat proprietor and Douglas Steam Ferries Ltd had to pay costs and damages. It is not recorded whether Capt Hampton of the *Rose* kept his job.

In 1899 the Harbour Commissioners were complaining about advertising for Beechams Pills displayed on the ferry boats, which was presumably against the terms of the lease. The board of Douglas Steam Ferries Ltd replied blaming their agent, who they said had overstepped his authority; but then promptly asked the Commissioners to vary to lease to allow the advertising to continue, as Mr Beecham had refused to release them from their contractual obligations.

In the second Balance Sheet, published in November 1898, the dividend was raised to 7½%, and a revenue of £185 was shown from advertising rents. On the same Balance Sheet a figure of £55 is shown as musicians rents – the appearance of musicians on the ferries lasted almost until the end of the service. The musicians income derived from gratuities and with a captive audience, in holiday mood, the ferries were obviously a sought after pitch. Each ferry carried a musician, a pianist – at least one photograph shows a piano on the open decks, an accordionist or a fiddler to entertain the passengers.

As a limited liability company, Douglas Steam Ferries Ltd were not obliged to show details of their financial accounts in the annual returns until 1921. One of the few clues to the success of the company was given in a newspaper report of the Annual General Meeting of the company in November 1901, when the directors reported that since the company took over the service in 1897 the ferries had carried 2,812,912 passengers. The fare was always 1d so the company had a gross income of some £11,720 over the same period.

The years from 1900 to the outbreak of the Great War were the zenith of the island's tourist industry and the Douglas Head ferries profited enormously from the huge annual influx of visitors.

The ferries ran from the root of Victoria Pier – which was at the south end of Douglas Promenade, near the terminus of the horse tramway and cable car systems – across Douglas Harbour to a set of steps at the inner end of the Breakwater, properly called the Battery Pier. At the top of the steps were two turnstiles with small pay booths, one for passengers going to Douglas Head and one for returning passengers. No fares were collected on board and none were collected at Victoria Pier, although in later years a combined ticket for the ferry, incline railway, Douglas Southern Tramway and Port Soderick funicular railway could be purchased in the Victoria Pier arcade.

DOUGLAS HEAD FERRY PASSENGER NUMBERS 1897 – 1901

1897	1898	1899	1900	1901
481562	549576	700854	512682	563038

On one Sunday in 1901 the ferries carried over 30,000 passengers.

The beginning of hostilities, in August 1914, quickly brought an end to the season and at a stroke removed the need for the ferry service. Exactly what happened to the ferry steamers during the Great War is obscure. It was thought that they were laid up at the top of Douglas Harbour on their traditional winter lay up berths. However, the Shipping Register for the Port of Douglas reveals a startling fact, that the *Thistle* sank on 23 November 1916, whilst on Admiralty Service off Aberdeen. What she was doing on the east coast of Scotland, or how she came to be there has not been traced. Her large passenger capacity and excellent manoeuvrability would have made her eminently suitable as a liberty boat in a sheltered anchorage.

The ferry service re-opened in 1919 with just two vessels, the *Rose* and the *Shamrock*, and continued in this manner until

Standing room only! Just about to sail from the Battery Pier in a picture taken between the wars. The steam ferry is moored outside one of the wooden landing barges introduced in 1919 which were moored at either end of the run to marshal passengers in readiness for embarkation and speed up the turnaround times.
STEPHEN DEARDEN COLLECTION

1926. In the 1919 Annual Report the Chairman, J. A. Brown, stated that the Directors had hesitated to order a replacement for the steamer *Thistle* which he stated was lost in the North Sea whilst in the service of the Imperial Government. They had managed to improve their boarding arrangements by employing two barges, moored at Battery Pier and Victoria Pier – they allowed waiting passengers to be marshalled on the barge and so avoid congestion on the piers and steps. At the same meeting it was reported that the Isle of Man Government had sanctioned an increase in Douglas Harbour ferry fares from 1d to 2d, a move which was beneficial to to the Douglas Head Ferry and other rowing ferries and waterman boats which were still in operation. The company was soon back in business and reported a profit for the year ending September 1919 of £1,738.11s.7d, rising to £2,667.4s.5d in 1921 when a 30% dividend was declared.

The second THISTLE *on her delivery voyage, sailing down the River Weaver from W. J. Yarwood's Northwich shipyard in 1926.* CLIVE GUTHRIE COLLECTION

The Thistle (1926) in service shortly after arrival.
STEPHEN CARTER COLLECTION

Mr. Richard Cain, who severed his association with the House of Keys in November, 1934, after representing Ayre Sheading for fifteen years, will long be remembered for his activities in championing the interests of agriculture. Is the managing director of the famous Castletown Brewery, chairman of the Steam Ferries, etc., etc.

A caricature of Richard Cain holding a Douglas Head Ferry steamer, published in a local magazine at the time of his retirement from the House of Keys – the Manx Parliament.
PETER KELLY COLLECTION

In 1925 the company ordered a new *Thistle* which was built by W. J. Yarwood on the River Weaver and was delivered under her own steam on 23 July 1926. The new vessel was similar but not identical to the original trio and was slightly larger, having a passenger certificate for 430 as opposed to the 350 of the three earlier vessels. It seems that the

Shamrock – possibly in a poor condition – was not much used after the arrival of the *Thistle*. Post war visitor numbers travelling to Douglas Head had shown a gradual decline, it would seem that only two ferries were now required. By the early 1930s the *Shamrock* was used only as a floating landing stage at Battery Pier.

Until the outbreak of the Second World

A general view across Douglas Harbour and Douglas Bay looking from Douglas Head. In the left hand foreground is the Camera Obscura, to the right and below the Douglas Head Incline Railway, and side show booths on Battery Flat (so called because there was originally a battery protecting Douglas Harbour from invasion by the French during the Napoleonic Wars). There are two steam cranes on Battery Pier. The Steam Packet's BEN MY CHREE, built by Cammell Lairds in 1927, is leaving the Victoria Pier, with another Steam Packet ship , the VIKING (1905), on the inside of the Pier. A Douglas Head steam ferry can just be seen at the inner end of the Victoria Pier, lying at the ferry steps, just above the Camera Obscura. the Douglas Head Ferry ran from there to Battery Pier ferry steps, which are situated just to the left of the left hand steam crane.

In Douglas Bay can be seen Conister Rock and the Tower of Refuge. This structure was built in 1832 from moneys raised by a public subscription started by Sir William Hillary and was designed as a shelter for sailors whose vessels were wrecked on the Conister Rock. When the Tower of Refuge was built the various piers that can be seen in the picture did not exist and the rock was in the way of the entrance to the original harbour. In the 1930s the seaward face of the Tower of Refuge was painted white after the Steam Packet's MONA ran aground on the rocks in thick fog.

STEPHEN CARTER COLLECTION

Douglas Harbour between the wars. A Douglas Head Ferry steamer can be seen at the Victoria Pier ferry steps, ahead of the Steam Packets MONA'S QUEEN – *built by Cammell Lairds in 1934, with other Steam Packet ships on the pier. In the middle ground on the far side of King Edward VIII Pier (which dates this photo to about 1937/8 as this pier is reputed to be the only public works in the country named during his brief reign before his abdication) are two Steam Packet ships, while the Liverpool and North Wales* ST SEIRIOL *is on the nearest side. Immediately astern of the* ST SEIRIOL *is the other Douglas Head Ferry steamer.* STEPHEN CARTER COLLECTION

War in 1939 the company continued to trade profitably, although the steadily reducing dividend payments, from 30% in 1921 to between 6% and 5% by the outbreak of war, was indicative that the Douglas Head Ferry trade was declining, as the traditional entertainments moved away.

In 1940 Douglas Steam Ferries Ltd sold the *Shamrock* for breaking, for £75, but her registry was not cancelled until 3 December 1942 when the Registrar of Ships received advice from Mr Wilfred Kissack Cain, described as the beneficial owner, that the vessel had been broken up.

During 1941 and 1942 no dividend declared at all, the company making a loss of £12.11s.8d

in 1942 and a profit of £306.14s.10d in 1943. Thereafter dividends resumed at 5% and 7½% until Douglas Steam Ferries Ltd ceased trading in 1948.

As the ferry was not running during the war how did they make a profit? Certainly the company had made some wise investments in Isle of Man Steam Packet and other shares, but the most likely cause of the return to profit was the chartering of the *Rose* and *Thistle* on war work. The ferry steamers were taken to Londonderry where they were used to land US forces arriving on troopships. Both vessels were returned after the war in a very poor condition, with bent and damaged bulwarks, the boiler of the *Rose* in particular having

Winter lay up in Douglas 1928/29. In the foreground, right to left: the Douglas Head ferry steamers: THISTLE, ROSE and SHAMROCK; and the Port Soderick boats KARINA, PEVERIL and MANNIN; and two unidentified launches. Behind, moored on the Tongue, are the bows of the Steam Packets' last paddle steamer MONA'S QUEEN. Moored on North Quay is Capt Ernest Jones' coal schooner' the EDITH MAY, in which he brought coal from Point of Ayre colliery, on the River Dee, and sold it around Douglas. His grandson runs the same coal business today – but not from the schooner. BY KIND PERMISSION OF MANX NATIONAL HERITAGE

suffered badly. They had been fitted with wheelhouses, no doubt because they had been in use winter and summer as opposed to the fairly cosseted summer existence they had enjoyed in Douglas. The 1946 annual returns have a note that the company was expecting payment from the British Government of £1249.11s.2d for repairs, no doubt towards the refurbishment costs of their Londonderry adventures.

Chapter Four
The final years

From its inception in 1897 to its demise in 1949 Douglas Steam Ferries Ltd had only five persons listed as Ships' Managers. This is an official position relating to requirements in the Merchant Shipping Acts for a person who shall be deemed responsible for legal and safe operation of the ship (as opposed to the master who controls the navigation and day to day operation on board the vessel). The managers were the first Company Secretary, William Horrocks, succeeded by Thomas Cannan Garrett of South Quay, Douglas in November 1913, then by the Chairman, John Archibald Brown in March 1918, then the next Chairman, Richard Cain, of St Helena, Spring Valley, Douglas on 18 January 1926. Richard Cain later organised the sale of the ferry steamers to a new company in 1948.

In the early years the company employed Capt McNamara as their Marine Superintendent but there is no record of how long this position remained. After the Second World War the two remaining ferries, the *Rose* and the *Thistle*, were laid up in Castletown Harbour. In August 1945 Edward Bryden Cannell's appointment as Ships' Manager marked the start of the next phase in the history of the Douglas Head Ferry.

Edward Cannell was a retired headmaster, a friend of Richard Cain, the Chairman of Douglas Steam Ferries Ltd. Cain suggested that Cannell's sons, Douglas and Cyril, might like to take over the operation of the Douglas Head Ferry and a tentative agreement was reached. Douglas Cannell was at this time a marine engineer in the Merchant Navy and his brother Cyril had served as a pilot in the RAF during the war. Between them they started work to refurbish the ferries which were still laid up in Castletown. Also laid up in Castletown were the two wooden barges that had been used as floating landing stages at the piers. In May 1949 the *Rose* and the *Thistle* were sold to a new concern, the Douglas Head Ferry Ltd which was incorporated on the 16 May 1949. Edward Cannell had died in December 1948 so the shareholders of the Douglas Head Ferry Ltd were Alice Victoria Maud Cannell, his widow, and Douglas and Cyril Cannell. The address of the new company was 2 North Quay, Douglas but in 1950 it was changed to the Shipyard, Peel,

The first post World War Two steaming of the THISTLE at Douglas in 1949. Note that the open bridge had been fitted with an enclosed wheelhouse during the war years. CYRIL AND DOUGLAS CANNELL

which the company had purchased as a base for refitting and over-wintering the vessels.

Douglas Steam Ferries Ltd went into voluntary liquidation and when it was finally wound up in 1950 the final distribution of funds was made to the shareholders. Shareholders received £1. 18s. 0d for each £1 share – which had only been paid up to 18 shillings in 1897. With the excellent dividends paid during the life of the company it had been, as they say, 'a nice little earner' for the shareholders.

The Cannells had both the *Rose* and the *Thistle* towed to Douglas by fishing boats, an operation which in itself caused problems as the tow ropes were old and kept parting, nearly losing one of the ferry steamers en-route. Once in Douglas they concentrated on a mechanical overhaul and then, early in 1949, both ferry steamers were moved to the gridiron in Ramsey Harbour, the *Thistle* now in steam, towing the *Rose*. They were there for inspection by both the Board of Trade, for their passenger certificates and Lloyds for the insurance. Whilst the *Thistle*, after some more work, eventually passed the surveys, the boiler on the *Rose* was condemned and she never steamed again. Both vessels returned to Douglas, once again the *Thistle* towing the *Rose*. The Douglas Head Ferry was restarted in the beginning of June 1949 using the *Thistle*. Rather than replace the boiler on the *Rose*, the Cannell brothers decided to convert her from steam to diesel and to this end obtained two

war surplus, unused, AEC 11.3 litre diesel engines. The steam machinery was removed but the conversion never took place. Apart from refurbishing the ferry steamers, the Cannell brothers had to build a new turnstile house at Battery Pier, the original buildings having been demolished during the war.

Although the ferry service was again busy as holiday makers returned to the island in their thousands, another problem suddenly appeared. Douglas Corporation, which owned a large and profitable municipal bus service as well as the horse tramway on Douglas Promenade, felt that they should control all public transport within the Town boundaries. The Corporation approached the Cannell brothers to see if they would sell the ferry but the Cannells' rejected their advances – shades of 1896. The Corporation then flexed its municipal muscle and opened a new bus route from the top of the ferry steps at Victoria Pier to the top of the ferry steps at Battery Pier, in a blatant attempt to take the trade from Douglas Head Ferry Ltd – not Douglas Corporation's finest hour. The Douglas Head Incline Railway had also restarted in 1949, and the open air theatre, the Camera Obscura and the Douglas Head Hotel were all very much back in business, and to a great extent dependent on passengers arriving on the ferries and incline railway. The Cannell brothers had received some assistance from the brewers Heron and Brearley and also from a local businessman, James Ritchie, who for

The inaugural sailing of Douglas Head Ferry Ltd in June 1949, with local dignitaries on board. In the foreground standing in front of the lifebuoy is Douglas Cannell, with the master Capt Moore in the wheelhouse. Note that to improve visibility the wartime windows have been removed and through the wheelhouse door can be seen the railway engine style reversing lever for one of the engines, which along with the extended main steam valve controls and the wheel enabled the master to have full control from the wheelhouse. This was used on the very earliest Douglas Head ferry steamers and allowed them to be controlled by one man, requiring only a stoker to complete the crew, who could also be on deck at times. This arrangement meant, however, according to Cyril and Douglas Cannell, that the master needed to be an octopus to man all the controls. CYRIL AND DOUGLAS CANNELL

Form St. 5.

In duplicate.

PASSENGER CERTIFICATE

For a ship plying in smooth water in estuaries and lakes.

Issued by the
MINISTRY OF TRANSPORT

Name of Ship _____ THISTLE

Owner, or Agent _____ The Douglas Head Ferries Limited.

Port of registry.	Official number.	Gross tonnage
DOUGLAS	145303	65

LIMITS BEYOND WHICH THIS SHIP IS NOT TO PLY.

In Douglas Harbour from Battery Pier to Victoria Pier

NUMBER OF PASSENGERS AND CREW.

Number of passengers.	Crew.	Total passengers and crew.
400	2	402

NOTE.—If any of the space measured for passenger accommodation is occupied by cattle or other animals, or by cargo or other articles, one passenger is to be deducted from the number stated above for every three square feet so occupied.

BOATS AND LIFE-SAVING APPLIANCES.

-	Boats capable of accommodating ... ... -	persons.
22	Buoyant apparatus capable of supporting 300	persons.
24	Lifebuoys.	
-	Life-jackets.	

THIS IS TO CERTIFY that the provisions of the Merchant Shipping Acts relating to the survey of passenger ships have been complied with, and that this ship is fit to ply within the limits and with the number of passengers stated above.

This certificate will remain in force, unless previously cancelled, until the 12th day of May, 1951.

Issued at the Ministry of Transport this 13th day of June, 19 50.

Examined and Registered.

One of these duplicate certificates is to be put up in a conspicuous place on board the ship where it will be legible to all persons on board, and to be so kept up and legible while the certificate remains in force and the ship is in use, under a penalty not exceeding TEN POUNDS.

If the number of passengers carried exceeds the number stated on this certificate, the master or owner will be liable to a penalty not exceeding TWENTY POUNDS, and to a further penalty for every passenger beyond the proper number.

The Board of Trade Passenger Certificate for the steam ferry THISTLE issued 13 June 1950.
CYRIL AND DOUGLAS CANNELL

many years held the catering contract for the Isle of Man Steam Packet. Both Ritchie and the brewery had a vested interest in the resumption of the ferry service. The Cannells wrote to the Corporation asking them to withdraw the bus service but this apparently fell on deaf ears. The Harbour Board then joined the fray by seeking to take out an injunction against the Corporation on the grounds that the latter did not have permission to operate a bus service on Harbour Board lands and roads. The Corporation countered by saying that they had authority to run buses anywhere within the Douglas Town boundaries. Whilst the legal arguments dragged on the buses continued to run.

In 1950 the ferry continued to operate using only the *Thistle*, but the price of coal was rocketing and the Harbour Board would not sanction an increase in the fares. On occasions the *Thistle* would venture out of the harbour and several evening cruises around Douglas Bay were undertaken.

On one occasion there was a visiting naval cruiser at anchor in the bay on a courtesy visit and during the afternoon, as was and still is the custom, was opened to the public. The Douglas boatmen ran trips to land passengers on the warship, and although they sold return fares, they were less inclined later in the day to pick up passengers and return them to shore. This led to the Harbour Master, Capt Hughie Doran, to ask the ferry company if the *Thistle* could pick up a large number of passengers who had been left stranded on board the cruiser by the non return of the other licensed Douglas boats. The *Thistle* had to make five runs to land all the stranded passengers, who of course were not inclined to pay any more money having already ostensibly paid a return fare on their outward journey.

On senior race day – the culmination of the fortnight's TT motorcycle races – in 1950, one of the Isle of Man Steam Packet's ships arrived early in the morning in Douglas, quickly discharged her passengers and then immediately sailed to anchor in Douglas Bay to allow other incoming ships to berth. Only when at anchor it was discovered that the stewards had forgotten to wake some passengers sleeping in cabins below, and so once again the *Thistle* came to the rescue and was sent out to pick up the passengers.

During the busy summer months, the crews of the Steam Packet ships would often ask the *Thistle's* crew to run a rope to the other pier to assist in shifting ship or sailing, a request to which the ferry crew always obliged. However, when wanting to travel to Liverpool on business Cyril Cannell approached the Isle of Man Steam Packet's management for a free ticket – he met with a stern rebuff.

During the 1950 season it became obvious that the pre war passenger figures were never going to be regained and that the *Thistle,* with her 400 passenger capacity and expensive coal fired steam machinery, was too costly for the

DOUGLAS HEAD

25th JUNE to 1st SEPTEMBER inclusive.
EVERY WEEKDAY at 11 a.m. and 3 p.m.
By arrangement with Ed. W. Jones.

HARRY ORCHID presents . . . .

THE DOUGLAS HEAD
SWANEE MINSTRELS

Admission to enclosure 6d. — Deck Chairs 6d.
SPECIAL NOTE.—In the event of wet weather MORNING Performances will be held in Villa Marina Royal Hall.—1/-

CAFE, CAMERA OBSCURA, AMUSEMENT ARCADES and INCLINE RAILWAY
Frequent Service of Buses from Victoria Pier.

Do Not Miss a Visit to this Famous Beauty Spot

A local newspaper advertisement for Douglas Head in 1950. It was around this time that Douglas Corporation established a bus service in opposition to the Douglas Head Ferry – no mention is made of the ferry service in the advert.
STEPHEN CARTER COLLECTION

operation. Luckily for Douglas Head Ferry Ltd, Pembrokeshire County Council were looking for a ferry to supplement the vessels in use on the Neyland Ferry at Milford Haven and the Cannells sold them the *Thistle*. She left Douglas on 14 October 1950, under tow of the Ridson Beasley tug *Topmast No 10*. However, the old ferry steamer never made it to Wales. At 7p.m., of the same day, she foundered in heavy seas, twelve miles south of the Skerries Lighthouse, Anglesey. The Cannell brothers felt that the tugmaster was in a hurry to sail and left in poor weather. The tug was considerably bigger than the *Thistle* and in their view the tug towed her under, steaming too hard in bad weather.

The Cannell brothers decided that the way forward was not to motorise the *Rose* but to replace the old double ended ferry boats with smaller motor launches, capable of being operated by a crew of two. Following the sale of the *Thistle*, Douglas Head Ferry Ltd bought three wooden motor launches. The largest, which they named *Thistle*, was an ex-US Navy harbour launch, purchased from the US base in Gareloch, Scotland. She was wooden, carvel built and 52 feet long. To facilitate quick embarkation and disembarkation the Cannells designed a small bridge deck over the engine compartment, with a small helm wheel. They had a Gareloch boatyard do this conversion work and fit one of the AEC engines, previously purchased for the *Rose*.

The *Shamrock* was a double diagonal hulled, 36 feet long ex-Royal Navy launch, purchased from the Navy Disposals Unit. The *Daffodil* was a clinker built, 36 feet long, ex-Royal Navy harbour launch, purchased from a pleasure boat operator in Pwllheli. Both were fitted with Kelvin Ricardo petrol/paraffin engines. The *Daffodil's* engine was later replaced with a Perkins P6 diesel and then a Vosper Ford petrol / paraffin. Both of these launches were fitted with a similar bridge deck to that on the *Thistle*.

The Cannells also bought the 26 feet long motor launch *Roma* – built originally for the Forresters of Port Soderick. Vincent Higgins skippered her on fishing trips from Douglas – later he skippered the larger *Thistle* on the Douglas Head Ferry.

The two old wooden landing barges, which it is thought had been built by Watsons' shipyard at Peel in 1919, were broken up and the *Rose* was reduced to a landing barge for use at Battery Pier.

At the end of the 1952 season the *Shamrock* was sold to the Stowell family of Douglas and used on the Port Soderick run.

At the end of the 1953 season the Cannells sold their interest in Douglas Head Ferry Ltd to Vincent Higgins and another Douglas boatman, George Kewley. They ran the *Thistle*, skippered by Vincent Higgins, exclusively on the Douglas Head Ferry. George Kewley ran the *Daffodil* to Port Soderick in the day, but helped out on the ferry at peak times.

Declining passenger numbers prompted them to sell the *Daffodil* in about 1955 to Bobby Ash, once again for use on the Port Soderick run. In 1955 George Kewley's shares were transferred to John Stanley Cooper of Douglas. He and Vincent Higgins continued running the *Thistle* on the Douglas Head Ferry until, in the mid 1960s, she was sold to John Clague, again for the Port Soderick run. Douglas Head Ferry Ltd was eventually struck off the Companies Register on 26 November 1975 for failing to submit returns for a number of years. The last of the old ferry steamers, the *Rose*, was laid up at the top of Douglas Harbour until cut up for scrap around 1967.

On board the THISTLE in 1950 heading for the Victoria Pier. BY KIND PERMISSION OF MANX NATIONAL HERITAGE

This was not quite the end however. Although Douglas Corporation had been running buses direct to Douglas Head since the 1950s there was still some ferry trade to be had. The open air theatre on Douglas Head was still in operation as was the Camera Obscura and the Douglas Head Hotel. On the sale of the *Thistle*, the then Douglas Lifeboat mechanic, a welshman named Peter Veale, bought a 36 seat wooden passenger launch the *Speedwell*, from the Swindlehurst family of Douglas. This vessel was a Kelvin launch, having been built and engined by the Bergius Kelvin Company of Glasgow and had been brought to the Island by John Clague in the early 1950s for use on the Port Soderick run. As lifeboat mechanic Peter Veale was not allowed to sail to Port Soderick but the RNLI did allow him to operate the Douglas Head Ferry route, because he would always be near the lifeboat house should an emergency occur and the lifeboat be needed. He continued to operate the ferry until the early 1970s when he left his position as lifeboat mechanic after obtaining a better paid job as an engineer at one of the Isle of Man Electricity Board's Power Stations. This really was the end of the ferry service.

In 1978 a new shipping company, Manx Line, opened the first roll-on roll-off service between Heysham and Douglas, and a new linkspan was installed at the inner end of the Victoria Pier across the ferry steps. In December of that year the linkspan was ripped from its moorings by a severe easterly gale and it virtually demolished the ferry steps. The subsequent repair obliterated them completely.

The Douglas Head Hotel has been converted into apartments and the Camera Obscura closed awaiting refurbishment for its

THE DAILY MAIL: THURSDAY, JULY 6, 1950

Wakes crowds join the Tynwald trek

THOUSANDS of lads and lasses from Bolton, Bury, and half a dozen other Lancashire cotton towns, holidaying at the Isle of Man, yesterday helped Manxmen to celebrate

A cutting from the DAILY MAIL, 6 July 1950, showing the holiday crowds aboard the THISTLE.
CYRIL AND DOUGLAS CANNELL

historical value. There is no requirement for a ferry to Douglas Head today.

To older members of the harbour community the steps on the Battery Pier are still the Ferry Steps, but these days the Harbour Authority positions a yacht mooring pontoon across them during the summer months.

Chapter Five
Onwards by sea to Port Soderick

Port Soderick is a small well-sheltered cove about three miles south of Douglas. Early in the nineteenth century there was a solitary fisherman's cottage on the beach. But by the 1880s the cove was subjected to commercial development.

The Crogga River runs into the cove and to the south of the river Henry Creetch built an Oyster Bar – he was the lessee of an oyster fishery in Port Soderick Bay. Oysters are not native to Manx waters and seed oysters were imported every season and laid out on the beds. There were also oyster beds between the Victoria Pier and the Tower of Refuge in Douglas Bay. Also involved in this venture was David Clarke, a Douglas builder and shareholder in Douglas Steam Ferries Ltd.

However, over the years the family that came to be the dominant force at Port Soderick was the Forresters. William Knox, creator of the Douglas Head Ferry, had been granted permission to build a pier at Port Soderick but never built it, and it was left to the Forresters to build the promenade and landing jetty. Port Soderick was a day-trip destination only, that is, there was no residential accommodation for visitors. Crowds of holidaymakers would arrive from Douglas every day. In its heyday Port Soderick was one of the busiest places on the Island. Visitors were brought by the Douglas Southern Electric Tramway which ran from Douglas Head to the top of the cliff above Port Soderick, and which in the boom years carried over 200,000 passengers a year. The Isle of Man Railway also carried many thousands and Port Soderick Station was one on the busiest on the line and of course many came by boat from Douglas.

At Port Soderick there were several cafés owned by different operators, a public house, a Camera Obscura, a glen, cliff walks and marine parades to view interesting rock formations, many of which were given names such as the Dragon Rock. There was an incline railway which connected the Douglas Southern Tram terminus to the Promenade, a sea lion pool, sideshows and stalls, musical entertainments, and last but by no means least, the feature which no self respecting Victorian or Edwardian seaside destination would be without, the Smugglers Caves.

The first large vessel to run to Port Soderick, the wooden built, twin screw, MERMAID of 1888, passing Douglas Head and towing a small wooden rowing boat – used to land passengers at Port Soderick before the slipway was constructed. BY KIND PERMISSION OF MANX NATIONAL HERITAGE

The Knox family were involved in the Douglas and Port Soderick Steamship Company and in 1888 they had built, at Watsons Shipyard at Peel, a fairly large, twin screw, passenger steamer, the *Mermaid*. Over 90 feet long with engines built by Knox's themselves, this vessel ran between Douglas and Port Soderick. The only known photograph shows her towing a large rowboat, which was used to land passengers onto the beach. The *Mermaid* carried around 200 passengers, and rowing such numbers ashore in a boat carrying no more than 20 passengers must have been a time consuming business. The *Mermaid* stopped running to Port Soderick in around 1900.

Many of the Douglas boatmen who hired out rowing boats from Douglas beach also operated sailing yachts carrying passengers to Port Soderick but it was the Forrester family once again who really dominated this trade.

Forrester's were credited as being the first boat owners on the Isle of Man to use motor vessels as opposed to steam or sailing vessels, for the carrying of fare paying passengers. From the early 1900s Thomas Forrester's two sons, Alexander Dickson Forrester and Thomas Henry Forrester owned a small fleet of motor launches – the *Roma*, *Finola* and the *Swastika* – named after the ancient symbol for peace. They also owned the rowing boats *Iona* and *Ina*, which were probably used to land passengers at Port Soderick before the landing jetty was built. In 1913 they took a

Forrester's launch SWASTIKA flying a White Ensign with naval personnel on board. It has long been the practice of local boatmen to charter launches to visiting naval vessels.
ANN PICKERING COLLECTION

Port Soderick slip in Edwardian times with Forrester's first ROMA alongside. ANN PICKERING COLLECTION

The *Karina* of 1913 dressed overall and anchored fore and aft in Port Soderick Bay as committee boat for a regatta. The launch *Peveril* and others are anchored in the background. Ann Pickering collection

giant leap forward and had built by Dickies of Tarbert, a well-known yacht building yard in Scotland, the passenger boat *Karina*. She measured over 50 feet long, was powered by a Gardner diesel engine, and was licensed by the Board of Trade to carry 67 passengers and three crew.

On 28 June 1913 the Forrester family incorporated Motor Launches Ltd with an authorised share capital of £5,000. Their four

motor and two rowing boats were sold to the new company for £3,000. Motor Launches Ltd mortgaged the new *Karina* to Parrs Bank Ltd of Prospect Hill, Douglas, for the same amount. This mortgage was discharged on 17 March 1922.

Motor Launches Ltd did not have long to enjoy its new vessel, as shortly after the outbreak of the Great War, in the following year, the *Karina* was chartered by the

The ROMA of 1921 when new, on trials with the Forrester brothers on board. ANN PICKERING COLLECTION

Admiralty and left the island bound for service as a picket boat at Scapa Flow. She remained at Scapa Flow for the duration of hostilities and was present when the surrendered German High Seas Fleet arrived. When de-commissioned in 1919, the *Karina* sailed back home via the Caledonian Canal with Alexander Forrester on board. She was fitted with a brass plate on the fore deck commemorating her naval service. The other motor boats stayed on the island and there is a picture of the *Swastika* carrying naval personnel and flying the White Ensign.

After the war, Port Soderick was again in full swing. Douglas boatmen began to exchange their sailing boats for twelve seater motor launches in the 1920s. In 1921/2 Motor Launches Ltd added another large craft to its fleet with a new *Roma*. She was a slightly smaller version of the *Karina*, and carried

The KARINA alongside Port Soderick slip between the world wars. Looking south showing the oyster beds, Cliff Cafe and stalls. ANN PICKERING COLLECTION

The KARINA towing the rowing ferry UMBRIA alongside about to pass through the swing bridge leaving Douglas inner harbour at the start of a days work. Astern of KARINA a Douglas trawler also awaits the opening of the bridge and the Isle of Man Harbour Board's dredger MANNIN built 1936 is moored on the North Quay. RICHARD DANIELSON COLLECTION

The KARINA, with awnings rigged, about to depart Port Soderick for Douglas. ANN PICKERING COLLECTION

The ROMA (1921) at Port Soderick. Looking north showing the hotel and pavilion, the swings, Marine Parade walkway and the incline railway connecting the resort to the Douglas Southern Electric Tramway which terminated on the headland. The incline railway had been bought second hand and was previously installed at the Falcon Cliff Hotel in Douglas. The small octagonal building in the foreground is a Camera Obscura of a different type to the one on Douglas Head. MARTIN BAIRSTOW COLLECTION

Passengers landing from the KARINA. Note the narrowness of the jetty and the rocks on the other side. The PEVERIL lies at anchor in the bay. BY KIND PERMISSION OF MANX NATIONAL HERITAGE

about 50 passengers. She had twin screws to assist in berthing alongside the tricky Port Soderick jetty. The small twelve seater motor launches were sold. Unfortunately both of Thomas Forrester's sons, Alex and Harry died young. Due to illness Thomas decided to sell off Port Soderick. Motor Launches Ltd sold the *Roma* and continued the *Karina* alone – the largest and most efficient revenue earner. Her skipper, William George Shimmin (known as Wally), was a capable skipper.

Unlike other Douglas boats, which plied for hire from Douglas Promenade, the *Karina* always sailed from the ferry steps on Victoria Pier. For many years, as well as owning Port Soderick, the Forrester's kept the large cafe in Victoria Pier Buildings, so their businesses were conveniently located.

At the outbreak of the Second World War in 1939, the *Karina* was again requisitioned. She was sailed from Douglas to Liverpool by Wally Shimmin. During the war the *Karina* served as a mine detection vessel in Liverpool Bay, something that her wooden construction and shallow draught made her ideally suited to. She was decommissioned at Dickies boatyard at Bangor in the Menai Straits and was sailed home in 1946 once again by Wally Shimmin. On return to Douglas a new 4LW Gardner engine was fitted and the Karina once again resumed her peacetime duties on the Port Soderick run.

Winter lay up in Douglas Harbour probably 1928 or 1929. The Isle of Man Steam Packet Company's last paddle steamer the MONA'S QUEEN *is laid up on the Tongue. Moored outside the paddler can be seen a Douglas Head steam ferry with one of the landing barges outside and the second wooden landing barge can be observed moored astern of the paddle box. In the foreground Forrester's motor launches* KARINA *and* ROMA *are laid up together with local passenger yachts.* STEPHEN CARTER COLLECTION

Port Soderick c.1952 with the launch SPEEDWELL alongside and the KARINA nosing in, no doubt wanting the smaller vessel to move off. This often caused friction between rival boatmen after the Forresters had sold the resort and the KARINA no longer had first call on the jetty. STEPHEN CARTER COLLECTION

In 1946 Wally Shimmin bought a majority shareholding in Motor Launches Ltd and thereby gained controlling interest in the *Karina* and a large rowing boat, the *Umbria* – used at low water spring tides to land passengers at Port Soderick. Wally Shimmin was the main pilot for the Port of Douglas, a position he had held since before the Second World War (pilots at that time were not licensed and to a certain extent it was a free for all trade).

In 1949 there were 192 licensed rowing boats, 16 licensed motor boats and 8 licensed rowing ferries in Douglas. Only the steam ferry *Thistle*, the *Karina* and the 8 rowing ferries were licensed to carry more than 12 passengers.

Until 1946 any passenger vessel operating on a Class 6 licence (vessels carrying more than twelve passengers, operating in fine weather, during the summer months and within a confined area of operation) had to be fully decked boats. Both the *Karina* and the *Roma* met this criteria. However, after this date the rules were changed and well decked boats were permitted to run between Douglas and Port Soderick. This opened up the Port Soderick station to many more boatmen.

The first newcomer was a 36 feet long ex-Admiralty launch, the *Skylark*, which was brought to Douglas by Jimmy and Donald Lindsay. She was licensed for 32 passengers, increased later to 47 passengers after adding extra safety equipment.

The *Skylark* was quickly followed by the similarly sized *Speedwell* – later to be the last Douglas Head ferryboat. She was operated by John Clague and later owned by the Swindlehurst family.

In the early 1950s a large motor fishing vessel, the *St Maughold*, owned by Pat Creer and Bob Corrin, was licensed for 67 passengers and put on the Promenade station, running to Port Soderick or to Laxey

Wally Shimmin, for many years master and later owner of the Karina, *and for over 30 years the main Douglas pilot.*

ANN PICKERING COLLECTION

The end of the day at Douglas Harbour. Wally Shimmin on the KARINA slips between a string of rowing boats which are being towed back to harbour after a day's hiring on Douglas Promenade. She passes the Ramsey Steamship Company's steam coaster BEN MAYE moored at the Coffee Palace berth and getting ready to sail after discharging. Alongside the KARINA is the rowing boat UMBRIA
RAMSEY STEAMSHIP COMPANY LTD

Bay. The *St Maughold*, however was too deep to go alongside Port Soderick jetty and passengers had to be landed by a small boat. The *St Maughold* also spent much time running milk in from Ireland as there was a shortage of locally produced milk at the time. Pat Creer, Bob Corrin together with fish merchant Alf Devereau, later purchased the ex-Douglas Head ferryboat *Shamrock* from the Stowell family and never licensed the *St Maughold* again.

Another boat to arrive on the scene at this time was the *Silver Foam*. She was built as a Blackpool beach boat and was lying derelict in Laxey Harbour until bought by a local boatman and Lifeboat Coxswain, Bobby Lee. The *Silver Foam* was rebuilt with a Kelvin engine and put on the Port Soderick run.

Douglas Head Ferry Ltd had purchased three motor launches in 1950: the *Thistle*; *Shamrock*; and the *Daffodil*; – these also ended up running to Port Soderick at various times.

By 1960 the Port Soderick run was catered for by the following vessels: *Karina, Daffodil, Shamrock, Silver Foam, Speedwell,* and *Rosemary* (ex-*Skylark*) – all Board of Trade boats licensed for more than twelve passengers. In addition there were the twelve seater boats: *Useful, Margaret Ann, Romany Rose, Peveril, Onward* and occasionally the *Glee Maiden, Redwing, Fisher Lass, Homarus, Colleen* and *Mannin*. The last named, the *Mannin,* which appeared briefly in the George

Advertising board on Douglas Promenade. The size of the boards was strictly controlled by Douglas Corporation as was the allocation of the various steps and stands on the Promenade. DAVID CORRAN

Formby film *No Limit,* began life as the Whitehaven sailing and pulling lifeboat. After RNLI service she was sold and had a Kelvin petrol paraffin engine fitted on Garwick Beach by Mr E. B. Christian. Not all the twelve seater boats ran to Port Soderick on a regular basis, many were engaged in angling trips in Douglas Bay, and made only occasional forays down the coast.

The DAFFODIL arriving at Port Soderick with a full load. The SHAMROCK, having discharged her Port Soderick passengers and left the jetty, is anchored in the bay with an angling party.
BOBBY ASH

Winter in the 1950s at Douglas. Launches laid up at the top of the harbour on the Bank. Left to right: unknown, REDWING, ROSEMARY, SHAMROCK, ONWARD. In the background the is ex-ferry steamer ROSE – then in use as a landing barge at the Battery Pier – with the motor ferry THISTLE alongside. JOHN HALSALL

By 1960 traffic for the *Karina* was declining. Before the Second World War she had been the only Port Soderick boat with a large passenger capacity sailing from Victoria Pier. However, the post war proliferation of motor launches on the Port Soderick station, operating from Douglas Promenade and beach, creamed-off many passengers before they even reached Victoria Pier. Wally Shimmin retired and in 1961 sold his shareholding in Motor Launches Ltd to Cecil Mark Watterson and his son Donald Watterson.

The Watterson's owned Groudle Glen and it was their plan to build a landing at Groudle and run the *Karina* there from Douglas. But the plan was never realised and after the 1961 season – during which the *Karina* was skippered occasionally by Alan Bridson, later a much respected Captain with the Isle of Man

Left to right: SPEEDWELL, COLLEEN, MARGARET ANN, ROMA. Behind: Colby Cubbins' steam yacht GLEN STRATHALLAN, the tug ANNIE, and the KARINA. Moored in the distance on the North Quay is the HOMARUS, while the PEVERIL lies outside the Harbour Board diving boat PERRAGH. JOHN HALSALL

Steam Packet Company – she was laid up at Castletown. In 1963 the *Karina* was issued with a licence to ply from Castletown or Port St Mary around the Calf of Man, but it is not known whether the vessel ever did any such trips. After further periods of lay up in Castletown and Peel the *Karina* was eventually sold off the Island to a Liverpool owner, Harold Hobson, who had been a regular passenger during the 1950s and admired the vessel. The *Karina* is now a private motor cruiser based at Port Penrhyn, North Wales.

The *Karina* had always been regarded as the most prestigious vessel on the Port Soderick run. Below decks – where the passengers were never allowed – she was fitted out and kept like a yacht. There was owner's accommodation aft with four bunks and a small washroom and toilet, forward was a small galley and crew's quarters, with the engine room in between. The *Karina* was unusual for a motor boat in that she was fitted with a long cast iron keel instead of a wooden keel and this was designed to give her the required stability for carrying passengers on deck.

At the end of the season the Forrester family would usually sail in the *Karina* to Scotland for a holiday. This tradition was continued after Wally Shimmin had bought the vessel. In the early 1950s he took the vessel to Scotland with several local business men on board; Doug Quirk of Quirks the Bakers, Keppel Shimmin the auctioneer, and others. It is thought that these businessmen had helped Wally to buy and re-engine the *Karina* after the war and certainly Keppel Shimmin had the use of Wally's small motor boat, the *Iona,* for a number of years during this period. Keppel's son Keith also worked for a time as deck boy on the vessel.

Wally sold the *Karina* after he had a mild heart attack, but he continued as pilot into the mid 1960s. When he finally retired he had been a pilot for over 35 years. Bobby Lee then took over as pilot. Latterly they used the *Silver Foam* as a pilot vessel. Wally had links back to the days of sailing schooners which still came to Douglas up to the Second World War, often bringing cargoes of timber. On the harbour bed underneath the old swing bridge was a heavy chain stretching from one side of the harbour to the other. This was a relic from sailing ship days, when, if they were travelling too fast with a following wind, they would

The SPEEDWELL, *a Kelvin built launch fitted, at this time, with her original Kelvin 13/15 petrol paraffin, two cylinder, poppet valve engine.* JOHN HALSALL

The PEVERIL *taking a catch of queen scallops off the fishing vessel* NORTH SCARLE, *which had run aground on the rocks at Port Soderick in fog in May 1976. The new Port Soderick Hotel is in the background. The* NORTH SCARLE *was subsequently pulled off but was so badly damaged that she was declared a constructive total loss. The* PEVERIL *at this time was owned by the author who is seen transferring the catch.* STEPHEN CARTER COLLECTION

drop a stern anchor to catch this chain to arrest their progress. In retirement Wally and his wife would take their car and sit up Douglas Head watching the comings and goings in the harbour. In the summer they also had another passenger on the outing – their budgie in a cage.

The normal departure times for Port Soderick from Douglas were 10 a.m. and 2 p.m. – most boats doing two runs a day in the season. As stated, the *Karina* ran from the ferry steps on Victoria Pier but the other boats worked off the Promenades, some from the steps on the Loch Promenade, moving to the

Block (local name for the Peveril Jetty) when the tide left the steps; whilst others worked off the beach. The owners of most of these launches also had fleets of rowing boats and the motor launches working from the beach, would anchor offshore while passengers were rowed out. Each launch had a boarding ladder which hooked over the rails to allow passengers to climb out of the rowing boat onto the launch. On the beach each owner had a landing stage, this was a contraption made up of heavy planks carried on two axles with four large diameter wooden handcart wheels. The stage would be pushed out into the water, up and down the beach to follow the tide. There was enough depth of water at the seaward end for rowing boats to get alongside. A long, springy, plank connected the landward end to the beach.

All the motor launches carried hand lines for fishing. On arrival at Port Soderick most of the passengers would disembark but some, who had paid a little extra, would stay on board. The launch would anchor in Port Soderick Bay for fishing. The catch was mostly codling, mackerel or calagh (coley), but Port Soderick often produced a good ling. At the due time the launch would up anchor and return to Port Soderick jetty to pick up the return passengers and any singles, of which there were often many. On returning from Port Soderick the boats would usually land the passengers either at the Block, or the ferry steps on the Victoria Pier.

Overloading was not uncommon and the Harbour Board's Boat Inspector kept a keen eye on the proceedings. Prosecutions were not unusual. The Harbour Board also operated a launch, the *Bridgeen*, during the 'fifties and 'sixties, manned by Connie Hayes, who also kept an eye on the rowing boats and launches. Before the war a young clerk in the Harbour Board, John McLean, who later rose to the top job to become Secretary of the Board, was often sent down to check passenger numbers. On one pleasant afternoon, while checking passengers disembarking at the Victoria Pier from the two Douglas Head Ferry steamers, he counted 1050 passengers getting off the two vessels – they had a licence to carry a total of 780 between them.

The Harbour Masters also operated 'The Spot'. On the inner end of the Victoria Pier facing Douglas Bay, was a large black board about four or five feet square, which was hinged in the middle so that one half closed over the other. It was normally left in the closed position. If the Harbour Master considered that the weather was too bad in the bay for the boats to be hired out, he would go to The Spot and open the sign so that a large yellow spot, about three feet in diameter, on a black background, was displayed and which could be observed by all the boatmen. If The Spot was showing then hiring had to stop. Remarkably, considering the fact that in those days none of the boats

The motor launch ROSEMARY arriving at Port Soderick slip in the 1950's.
FREDDY KELLY COLLECTION

had radio communications there were very few accidents and boatmen were adept at watching and anticipating the movements of the Steam Packet and other ships. They were equally adept in anticipating the probable location of the duty Harbour Master when overloaded and would go to great lengths to land passengers away from his gaze.

All the boatmen have tales of amusing incidents which occurred over the years, but your author here relates one as an example. In the mid 1960s, during the school holidays, the author was mate and then skipper of the launch *Rosemary* running to Port Soderick. The *Rosemary* would be anchored off Broadway, further along the Promenade, where the boss, Lo Kelly, would be selling tickets for the afternoon's sailing. The author, then sixteen years old, picked up a family – mother, father and two sons – in a rowing boat from the wheeled stage and rowed them out to the anchored launch. On coming

Advertising boards for the ROSEMARY with the owner J L (Lo) Kelly on the left and skipper Jack Raby on the right
FREDDY KELLY COLLECTION

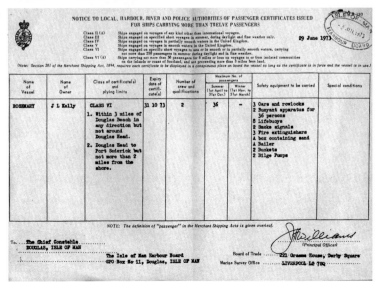

The Passenger Certificate of the motor launch ROSEMARY while she was owned by Lo Kelly. Later, after Bobby Christian bought her, the passenger capacity was increased to 47, by the addition of extra life saving apparatus
STEPHEN CARTER COLLECTION

Douglas boatmans annual outing. An event in the 1950' taken at the entrance to Glen Helen with its pub and Swiss Chalet cafe. FREDDY KELLY COLLECTION

alongside the launch it had to be explained to the passengers that to climb onboard the launch they had to hold the launch's handrails with both hands and simultaneously step onto the bottom rung of the ladder taking care not to push the rowing boat away from the side of the launch. This operation was successfully conducted many times every day, without incident. The father and two sons made the transfer without problem but the mother, who appeared to my youthful eyes, to be a lady of generous proportions, clothed in one of those flowery dresses popular at the time, was somewhat nervous. Although she managed to grasp the handrails of the motor launch, her feet seemed disinclined to leave the rowing boat with the inevitable result that the two vessels started to drift apart and nothing I could do seemed to check this drift. Next, the lady suddenly let go of the handrails and because she was by this time leaning well over the side of the rowing boat, the boat rolled and, splash, into the water she went.

What a commotion! Everybody in the launch was shouting, Lo Kelly on the beach was shouting and as you might imagine the lady was none too happy either. Try as I might, every time I tried to get her back into the rowing boat it nearly capsized, so, with a masterly bit of lateral thinking on my part, I managed to get her around to the stern of the boat and told her to hold onto the transom with both hands. I then rowed back to the shore towing the lady behind and deposited the unfortunate person in the shallow water, something akin to a beached whale. Luckily none the worse for her swim. Lo Kelly sent me back out to the motor launch to collect her husband and children and bring them ashore, but, as if to rub salt in the wound, the father having realised that his wife seemed perfectly alright, sent me back with the message that as his wife hadn't wanted to go in the first place, she could return to their lodgings on the Esplanade to get dry. He would not disappoint the sons and would go to Port Soderick without her. Imagine the litigation that might ensue if the same thing happened today.

As tourism declined in the 1960s the number of licensed boats fell away one by one. After the *Karina* the next to go was the *Shamrock*, which had been operated since the Douglas Head Ferry days by Pat Stowell and then by the partnership of Pat Creer, Bob Corran, and Alf Devereau. She was sold to Henry Crellin of Port St Mary who ran a diving business. The *Daffodil* changed hands several times, from the Ashe family to Jack Corran, then to Rodney Kennish whose family had, for many years operated the twelve seater *Peveril*. She was next sold to Ian Quirk and Bob Peel who used the vessel for whelk fishing. The *Thistle* was sold in the mid-1960s by Douglas Head Ferry Ltd to John Clague, who renamed her *Mary Ann* and ran her for a few years to Port Soderick. The *Mary Ann* made the headlines in a national Sunday tabloid when she had to be rescued by Douglas Lifeboat after an engine failure off Little Ness in bad weather. Not just full of passengers, she was overloaded, with 80 on board, her certificate allowed for only 64. She too was sold out of the passenger trade as a private angling boat. John Clague then bought a smaller launch, the *Laura*, licensed for 36 passengers, which he ran to Port Soderick in the 1970s. Latterly the Douglas Head ferry was run by Peter Veale with the *Speedwell*, until this vessel too was sold as a private angling boat at Peel, and eventually disappeared without trace on a delivery voyage after having been sold to Ireland, both of the crew being lost. The *Silver Foam*, one of the smallest Board of Trade boats, owned by Bobby Lee, was fitted with a succession of engines and lasted well into the early 1980s carrying passengers. On Bobby Lees' death in harness – he had a heart attack in his popper (a small unlicensed motor boat used for towing strings of rowing boats between the harbour and promenade) whilst towing his rowing boats out for a day's hire – she was owned for a short time by Bobby Lees' right hand man and the vessel's skipper Bob Jones. After a further couple of seasons it was bought by Frank Shimmin. It was never licensed again and only used as a popper. Bobby had followed Wally Shimmin as pilot and the *Silver Foam* was, for many years, used as the pilot boat at Douglas. J. L. Kelly, known as Lo, bought the *Skylark* from Don Lindsay and renamed it *Rosemary,* after his daughter. When he retired he sold his boating business to Bobby Christian, who continued to run the boat well into the 1980s as 'Fletcher Christian's Boats'. The *Rosemary* was eventually broken up at the top of Douglas Harbour.

Of the smaller boats, the *Peveril* was built for the Swindlehurst family in Circular Road, Douglas in the 1920s (some distance from the sea), mainly from timber salvaged from a wrecked schooner. She was operated for many years by John 'Tinnie' Kennish with his son Rodney as skipper. The Kennish family kept their rowing boats at Laxey during the winter and had one of the biggest fleets. At the end of the season the *Peveril* would tow the rowing boats to Laxey and return at the start of the following summer – it was an odd sight to see the *Peveril,* with a string of empty rowing boats, sailing up or down the coast to

Bobby Lee was coxswain of Douglas Lifeboat and followed Wally Shimmin as the Douglas pilot. For a great many years he owned the SILVER FOAM, *a former Blackpool beach boat, pictured during a quiet spell having a bottom clean on Douglas foreshore. It was common practice in fine weather to pull up a few rowing boats to do minor repairs or clean the bottom on the beach during quiet hiring out periods. Bobby also owned a fleet of rowing boats and several larger fishing vessels. He was awarded the British Empire Medal for his long and meritorious service as lifeboat coxswain.*
STEPHEN CARTER COLLECTION

Laxey. She was sold in the early 1970s to Albert Shimmin and then to the author, and was eventually broken up in 1980. The *Onward* was sold by Pat Stowell as a private pleasure boat in Ramsey and survives in a barn on Andreas Airfield. The *Romany Rose* (ex-*Roma [1]*) spent nearly 20 years out of the water on top of the Tongue in Douglas before being put back in the water and used privately. Readshaws' *Margaret Ann,* one of the last passenger boats to have a 13/15 Kelvin petrol paraffin engine, is still in existence as a private pleasure boat in Ramsey owned by Wilf Young.

For a gap of over twenty years there were no licensed passenger boats running to Port Soderick, Indeed, for a time, the only licensed boat in Douglas was the twelve seater *Girl Mary,* owned by General Marine Services and then the Laxey Towing Company Ltd. The *Girl Mary* also doubled as pilot boat,

Laxey Towing Company Ltd's launch Hopeful Lad *leaving Douglas Promenade for a combined Port Soderick and fishing trip.*
Stephen Carter collection

a role the vessel fulfils to this day. After 1992 it was used only occasionally on angling trips and never went to Port Soderick. Laxey Towing Company Ltd's first licensed passenger

boat, the *Hopeful Lad*, did do some trips to Port Soderick in 1978 but with a licence for just twelve passengers angling parties were more profitable. In September 2000 the Laxey

The KARINA in a former guise as the EASTERN BELLE of the Millbrook Steamboat & Trading Co Ltd. She is pictured in Plymouth's Sutton Pool where she originally plied as the ferryboat MAY QUEEN, for the Oreston & Turnchapel Steamboat Co Ltd – those villages being on the opposite shore of the River Plym. ALAN KITTRIDGE

Towing Company Ltd purchased a 100 seat ex-Plymouth ferryboat, the *Totnes Princess*. They brought the vessel to Douglas and renamed her *Karina*. She commenced running trips between Douglas and Port Soderick in the summer of 2001. Trips are also run to Laxey Harbour and Derbyhaven Bay. At 65 feet long the present *Karina* is probably the largest vessel ever to land at Port Soderick slip.

Unfortunately Port Soderick has suffered a similar decline to the pleasure boats. It was bought by Douglas Corporation in 1956 and

they spent much money rebuilding the resort. The Corporation sold the property in 1985 and it has since had a succession of owners. At the time of writing Port Soderick is again up for sale. The public house, now named the Anchor, has not opened for the 2002 season.

Laxey Towing Co Ltd's KARINA arriving at Laxey from Douglas in July 2003. ALAN KITTRIDGE

The *KARINA* (1913) in her present guise as a motor yacht. She is still fitted with the 4LW Gardner engine which was installed after the Second World War by Wally Shimmin. Pictured in autumn 2002 at Port Penrhyn, North Wales.

The present *KARINA* backs away from Douglas Promenade with the Tower of Refuge in the background. JOHN LUXTON

Details of vessels

DOUGLAS HEAD FERRY BOATS

Lancashire Lass
Description: Wooden, single screw, steam launch-tug.
Owned: William Knox and occasionally used on the Douglas Head Ferry.

Manx Lass
Description: Wooden, single screw, steam launch,
Owned: William Knox and used on Douglas Head Ferry.

Jumbo
Description: Wooden, double ended, single screw, steam ferry,
Owned: William Knox and used on Douglas Head Ferry.
Built: c.1883.

Jingo
Description: Wooden, double ended, twin screw, steam ferry.
Owned: William Knox and used on Douglas Head Ferry.
Built: c.1884.

Sambo
O.N.   (official number) 95754.
Description: Wooden, double ended, twin screw, steam ferry.
Owned: William Knox.
Built: 1890 by Qualtroughs Shipyard, Douglas Bridge.
Dimensions: 54 feet long x 16 feet wide x 6.3 feet deep. 38.95tg (tons gross), 20.20tn (tons net). Length of engine room 20 feet.
Engine: Two cylinder, compound, inverted. One boiler Built by Knox. .
Notes: Sold 21 July 1902 to Isle of Man Harbour Commissioners.
Registry closed 16 November.
1925 – used as a floating platform only, registry no longer required.

Rose
O.N. 108855.
Description: Steel, double ended, twin screw, steam ferry.
Owned: Douglas Steam Ferries Ltd.
From 28 May 1949 by Douglas Head Ferries Ltd.
Built: 1897 by the Dee Shipbuilding and Engineering Co, Queensferry, Flint.
Dimensions: 59 feet (66 feet overall) x 18 feet x 6 feet. 48.80tg.
Engine: Two cylinder, compound, inverted, surface condensing.
Built by Tendall & Co, Hull.
Certificate: 350 passengers within Douglas Harbour.
Broken up at Douglas c.1970.

Shamrock
O.N. 108856.
Description: Steel, double ended, twin screw, steam ferry.
Owned: Douglas Steam Ferries Ltd.
Built: 1897 by the Dee Shipbuilding and Engineering Co, Queensferry, Flint.
Dimensions: 59 feet (66 feet overall) x 18 feet x 6 feet. 48.80tg.
Engine: Two cylinder, compound, inverted, surface condensing.
Built by Tendall & Co, Hull.
Certificate: 350 passengers within Douglas Harbour.
Notes: Broken up at Douglas 1942.

Thistle
O.N. 108857.
Description: Steel, double ended, twin screw, steam ferry.
Owned: Douglas Steam Ferries Ltd.
Built: 1897 by the Dee Shipbuilding and Engineering Co, Queensferry, Flint.
Dimensions: 59 feet (66 feet overall) x 18 feet x 6 feet. 48.80tg.
Engine: Two cylinder, compound, inverted, surface condensing.
Built by Tendall & Co, Hull.
Certificate: 350 passengers within Douglas Harbour.
Notes: Sank off Aberdeen 23 November 1916 whilst on Admiralty service. Register closed 22 March 1918.

Note: The above three vessels were listed as being steel-built but were in fact constructed of lowmoor iron, a commonly used material at the time and very resistant to corrosion.

Thistle

O.N. 145303.

Description:	Steel, double ended, twin screw, steam ferry.
Owned:	Douglas Steam Ferries Ltd.
	Sold to Douglas Head Ferries Ltd on 28 May 1949.
Built:	1926 (launched 29 June 1926) by W. J. Yarwood, Northwich, Cheshire.
Dimensions:	54 feet (65 feet overall) x 22.6 feet x 6.9 feet. 67tg. 37tn.
Engine:	Two cylinder, compound, inverted engines, by builder. Horsepower 24 nominal, 65 brake and 76 indicated.
Certificate:	430 passengers within Douglas Harbour (later reduced to 400).
Notes:	Sold to Pembrokeshire County Council 12 October 1950.
	Lost under tow of tug *Topmast No 10* off Anglesey 14 October 1950.

Thistle

Description:	Wooden, carvel built, open launch, single screw.
Owned:	Purchased by Douglas Head Ferries Ltd in 1951.
Built:	US Navy picket boat
Dimensions:	52 feet x 13 feet x 5 feet.
Engine:	Originally fitted with US Chrysler Crown petrol engine.
	Re-engined on purchase with an AEC 11.3 diesel and later by a Perkins P 6 diesel removed from Douglas Bay passenger speedboat *Cuma*.
Certificate:	88 passengers on Douglas Head Ferry, 64 passengers to Port Soderick.
Notes:	Sold c.1965 to John Clague, Queen Street, Douglas and renamed *Mary Ann*.

Shamrock

Description:	Wooden, double diagonal, Royal Navy harbour launch, single screw.
Owned:	Purchased in 1951 by Douglas Head Ferries Ltd from the Navy Small Craft Disposals Unit.
Built:	Refitted at Peel Shipyard.
Dimensions:	36 feet x 11 feet x 5 feet.
Engine:	Originally fitted with Kelvin Ricardo petrol paraffin engine.
	Fitted with a Ford diesel 1954.
Certificate:	48 passengers.
Notes:	Sold 1952 to P. Stowell.

Sold 1954 to R. Corran, P. Creer and A. Devereau.
Sold c.1964 to H .Crellin Port St Mary.
Broken up Port St Mary c.1970.

Daffodil

Description:	Wooden, clinker built, Royal Navy harbour launch, single screw.
Owned:	Purchased 1951 by Douglas Head Ferries Ltd from a pleasure boat operator in Pwllheli.
Built:	Refitted at Peel Shipyard.
Dimensions:	36 feet x 11 feet x 5 feet.
Engines:	Originally fitted with a Kelvin Ricardo petrol paraffin engine.
	1954/5 Fitted with a Ford Vosper petrol paraffin engine.
	1964 fitted with Lister Blackstone diesel.
Certificate:	50 passengers.
Notes:	Sold 1954/5 to R. Ashe, Douglas.
	Sold 1964 to J. J. Corran, South Quay, Douglas.
	Sold 1973 to R. Kennish, Peveril Terrace, Douglas.
	Sold 1976 to I. Quirk and R. Peel as a fishing boat.
	Broken up Douglas c.1980.

PORT SODERICK BOATS

Mermaid

Description:	Wooden, twin screw, steamship.
Owned:	Douglas and Port Soderick Steamship Company.
Built:	1888 by Watson of Peel
Dimensions:	Length overall 88 feet x 17 feet beam. 80tg. 43tn.
Engines:	Two cylinder, compound, by Knox. Cylinders 10 inches and 20 inches x 14 inches stroke.
	One boiler by Lyndsay Burnett and Co, Glasgow.
Notes:	Register closed 7 November 1911 after she was lost in Irish Sea.

Karina

O.N. 118607.

Description:	Wooden, decked, single screw, motor launch.
Owned:	A. D. and T. H. Forrester.
	Sold to Motor Launches Ltd 1913.
Built:	1913 by Dickies of Tarbert.
Dimensions:	Length overall 52.6 feet x 12.6 feet beam.

	20.93tg 11.16tn.
Engine:	4 cylinder Gardner oil engine.
	1946 fitted with Gardner 4LW diesel engine 48 BHP.
Certificate:	Last licensed in 1963 for 67 passengers.
Notes:	25 March 1969 sold to Harold George Hobson of Liverpool.
	Currently (2002) owned by Bruce Stafford of Manchester and based at Port Penrhyn, Bangor, North Wales as a private pleasure boat.

Roma
O.N. 162400.

Description:	Wooden, decked, motor launch. Twin screw.
Owned:	Motor Launches Ltd.
Built:	1921 by Winram of Liverpool.
Dimensions:	48 feet x 11 feet x 5.1 feet. 18tg. 12tn.
Engine:	2 Atlantic petrol paraffin engines.
Certificate:	50 passengers.
Notes:	Sold 1934 to C. H. Martin of Blundlesands.
	By 1953 she was with Joseph McKee, Bridge Marine Works, Walton Bridge, Shepperton Middlesex.

Skylark

Description:	Wooden, carvel built, Royal Navy harbour launch.
Owned:	Purchased 1949 by J. Lindsay and D. Lindsay from J. Bolson & Sons, Poole.
Dimensions:	36 feet x 11 feet x 5 feet.
Engines:	Kelvin F 4 Ricardo petrol paraffin engine.
Certificate:	36 passengers.
Notes:	Sold 1952 to J. L. Kelly and renamed *Rosemary*.

Speedwell

Description:	Wooden, carvel built, open launch.
Owned:	J. Clague of Queen Street, Douglas.
Built:	Bergius Kelvin Co of Glasgow.
Dimensions:	32 feet x 9.5 feet x 4 feet.
Engine:	Kelvin 13/15 petrol paraffin engine.
	1959/60 Fitted with Ford 50 BHP diesel.
Certificate:	36 passengers.
Notes:	Sold 1959/60 to J. Swindlehurst of Douglas.
	Sold to Peter Veale c.1965 for use on Douglas Head Ferry.
	Sold privately c.1975 to Peel and then to Ireland.
	Lost with both crew members on delivery voyage to Ireland.

Silver Foam

Description:	Wooden, clinker built, open launch.
Owned:	Bought c.1952 by Robert Lee of Douglas as a wreck in Laxey Harbour.
Built:	as a Blackpool beach boat.
Dimensions:	32 feet x 10 feet x 4 feet.
Engine:	Fitted with Kelvin 13/15 petrol paraffin engine to replace original Atlantic engine.
	c.1965 fitted with Turner twin diesel engine.
	1967 fitted with BMC Morris Commodore diesel engine.
Certificate:	36 passengers.
Notes:	Robert Lee died in 1980 and the boat passed to Bob Jones of Douglas.
	Sold in 1981 to Frank Shimmin and not licensed.
	The *Silver Foam* lasted until 1990 after which it was sold for the engine which was fitted into the ex-Harbour Board launch *Bridgeen*.

St Maughold

Description:	Wooden, carvel built, motor fishing vessel.
Owned:	Owned by P. Creer, R. Corran and A. Devereau.
Built:	James Nobles of Fraserburgh in 1947.
Dimensions:	49 feet x 17 feet x 6 feet.
Engine:	60 HP McLaren.
Certificate:	67 passengers.
Notes:	Only used on passenger work for two seasons but remained in the Corran family for many years as a fishing boat.
	At present in Castletown as a private pleasure boat.

Rosemary

Description:	Ex-motor launch *Skylark*. Wooden, carvel built, Royal Navy harbour launch.
Owned:	J. L. Kelly of Douglas.
Dimensions:	36 feet x 11 feet x 5 feet.
Engines:	Fitted with Ford diesel engine.
Certificate:	47 passengers.
Notes:	Sold to R. E. Christian of Douglas c.1976.
	Broken up at the top of Douglas Harbour about 1990.

Mary Ann

Description:	Ex-motor launch *Thistle* – wooden, carvel built, open launch, single screw.
Owned:	J. Clague of Douglas.
Built:	US Navy picket boat
Dimensions:	52 feet x 13 feet x 5 feet.
Engine:	Perkins P 6 diesel removed from Douglas Bay passenger speedboat *Cuma.*
Certificate:	88 passengers on Douglas Head Ferry, 64 passengers to Port Soderick.
Notes:	Sold 1972 to F. Jones of Peel, Sold c.1978 to E. Craine and T. Miller as a fishing boat.

Laura

Description:	Wooden, carvel built, motor launch.
Owned:	Purchased from Northern Ireland by J. Clague in 1973.
Dimensions:	32 feet x 10 feet x 5 feet.
Engine:	Lister Blackstone diesel engine.
Certificate:	36 passengers
Notes:	Used for one or two seasons. Sold to J. Mallon of Douglas, renamed *Lily Margaret* and used as a fishing boat. Eventually broken up at Douglas.

Karina

Description:	Wooden, saloon, passenger ferry.
Owned:	Laxey Towing Co Ltd
Built:	Philip & Sons, Dartmouth in 1946.
Dimensions:	65 feet x 14.5 feet x 6 feet. 20tg. 11tn.
Engine:	Gardner 6LXB 127 HP marine diesel.
Certificate:	100 passengers.
Notes:	Built as the *May Queen* for the Oreston and Turnchapel Steamboat Co Ltd of Plymouth. Sold to Millbrook Steamboat & Trading Co Ltd and renamed *Eastern Belle* in 1956. Sold to Dart Pleasure Craft Ltd in 1978. Sold Riddalls of Dartmouth in 1989 and renamed by them *Totnes Princess.* Still in service 2003.

List of motor launches carrying up to twelve passengers and licensed by the Isle of Man Harbour Board and its successors. Many of these vessels changed hands frequently and most did trips to Port Soderick:

Colleen
Roma (Romany Rose)
Fisher Lass
Sea Fisher
Redwing
Homarus
Glee Maiden
Margaret Ann
Peveril
Onward
Useful
Mannin
Kathleen
Finola
Swastika
Hopeful Lad
Pisces
Morning Star
Girl Mary
Kitty

Acknowledgements

In compiling this small volume I have drawn on a number of sources. The majority of factual information has been gleaned from records and newspapers held by the Manx Museum and the staff of the Museum reference library have been a very great help, especially in locating some of the more obscure records from within the museums archives. The Museum has also provided many of the photographs used in the book. The brothers Douglas and Cyril Cannell who took over the Douglas Head Ferries after the war contributed a fund of knowledge as well as their photographs. The Port Soderick story would have been much poorer had it not been for the reminiscences and photographs of Miss Ann Pickering, grand daughter of the Forrester family, who was brought up a Port Soderick and sailed many times on the Karina with Wally Shimmin. Other members of the Islands maritime community who have contributed both photographs and reminiscences have included retired Chief Harbour Master for the Isle of Man, Captain David Cowell, former boatmen Bobby Ash senior and his son Bobby Ash, Bobby (Fletcher) Christian, David Corran, John Halsall, the late Rodney Kennish, George Kewley, Derrick (Mo) Mills, Bobby Pope, Louis and Freddy Kelly and Frank Shimmin. Other photographs and information were supplied by Martin Bairstow, Steven Dearden, Clive Guthrie, Peter Kelly, Alan Kittridge, John Luxton, Michael Messenger, Brian Quirk and Keith Shimmin. Richard Danielson, a maritime author of some repute, was kind enough to read the drafts and his help and encouragement has been much appreciated.

Index of passenger vessels

m.v. Karina

Step Aboard
and
Step Back in Time

Cruises from Douglas
to Laxey
Port Soderick and Derbyhaven

General Index